© Copyright 2016, Cynthia Mackey

All Rights Reserved

No part of this book may be reproduced, stored in a retrieval system, or transmitted by any means, electronic, mechanical, photocopying, recording, or otherwise, without written permission from the author.

ISBN: 978-1-943767-72-4

Katie Shaeffer, Pancake Maker

Written by Cynthia Mackey

Illustrated by Paula Nasmith

Katie Shaeffer loved building things, she loved collecting things, and most of all she loved pancakes.

"May I make pancakes today?" she asked her mother every morning.

"Well," said her mother, "You're too young to use the stove by yourself."

"Yes," said Dad, "Wait until you're older."

Katie sighed.

Katie imagined the day when she would finally make her very own pancakes…

"Maybe I can't use the stove," said Katie. "But I can build things."

As Katie cut the windows and doorways for her castle, she couldn't help thinking about the pancakes. She smiled. "What if I can use a little magic to make my pancakes?" she said to her toy horse.

Katie glued several bright buttons onto the cardboard. She attached shiny tin cans with some sticky tape and she balanced a few bright orange traffic cones on top.

"All my castle needs is just one more traffic cone right… Oh no!" cried Katie.

CRASH! It tumbled over, landing in a jumble like a junkyard mess. "I can't make pancakes; I can't even build things… but I can collect things!"

Katie searched for more treasures to add to her collection all the while thinking about those perfect pancakes and that little bit of magic she needed to make her dream come true.

Katie noticed the new boy in the neighbourhood. "Hey, look what I found!" Katie said to the boy. "Hi, I'm Baxter," he said. "Hi Baxter! I'm Katie and I can collect things, I can build things, and I just know I can make pancakes. One day I'm going to make…

Golden brown, fluffy as a cloud, perfectly round, PANCAKES!

And everyone will call me Katie Shaeffer, Pancake Maker." "Here Katie Shaeffer you can use some of these left over cartons for your next project," said Baxter. "Hey, thanks Baxter," said Katie. "Want to come over to my house?"

Katie showed Baxter her gigantic collection box. "Wow! What a pile of paraphernalia," said Baxter.

Katie's collection box was filled with corrugated cardboard, rainbow-coloured ribbon, spools, shiny tin cans, bright orange traffic cones, masking tape, popsicle sticks, plumbing pipes, billions of buttons, and kitchen gadgets, like tired toasters, mixing bowls, and even an old electric egg beater.

"I'm going to use it to build a pancake machine!" said Katie with excitement.

"If it really works, we'll have…

Golden brown, fluffy as a cloud, perfectly round, PANCAKES!"

Katie assembled and constructed; she glued and she taped; she stacked and she hammered, until finally her creation was done.

"I know just what these pancakes need," said Katie. "A little bit of magic!" Katie carefully poured some milk and delicately cracked two eggs into the machine. Baxter attentively added some oil, some flour, and a bit of salt.

"Now for the magic ingredient!" said Katie. And with golden fluffy pancakes in mind, she added a spoonful of baking powder, flipped the switch, waited a few minutes, and out came...

Golden brown,
fluffy as a cloud,
perfectly round,
PANCAKES!

"Wow!" shouted Baxter. "Amazing!" cheered Katie. "Just call me Katie Shaeffer, Pancake Maker!" Baxter tasted a pancake. "These pancakes are delicious aaaaaaaaand nutritious!" cried Baxter. "I know just what we need now!" said Katie.

Katie and Baxter walked to the store. They bought yellow butter, almond butter, and apple butter. They bought strawberry syrup, maple syrup, and buttermilk syrup. They bought raspberry jam, blueberry jam, and blackberry jam.

Katie and Baxter hurried home.

Just then they heard a clamorous commotion. "Oh, no!" they both shouted at once. "We forgot to turn the machine off!"

That marvelous machine was still making pancakes. There were pancakes on the ceiling, pancakes on the floor, pancakes on the bed, pancakes rolling out the door.

"Even we cannot eat that many pancakes," admitted Baxter.

"We can't eat all those pancakes, but we can have a party!" said Katie with a smile.

The aroma of warm pancakes wafted through the air. People started lining up for pancakes. Dad proudly announced, "Katie Shaeffer, you really are a pancake maker." Right behind her Mom and Dad were all of their neighbors and right behind their neighbours were all their friends. The pancakes were so delicious that everyone invited MORE friends. And they all loved the...

Katie took a bow.

"Just call me Katie Shaeffer, Pancake Maker!"

How to make your own
Golden brown,
fluffy as a cloud,
perfectly round
PANCAKES!

Katie's Perfect Pancakes
1 egg
1 cup all purpose flour
3/4 cup milk
1 tablespoon sugar
2 tablespoons vegetable oil
3 teaspoons of baking powder
1/2 teaspoon salt

Beat egg until fluffy. Add remaining ingredients and beat until smooth. Grease heated griddle if necessary. For each pancake pour about 3 tablespoons of batter from the tip of a large spoon. Use a pancake mold to make your pancakes perfectly round. Cook pancakes until puffy and dry around the edges. Flip and cook other side until golden brown.

For blueberry pancakes stir in 1/2 cup fresh blueberries.